GODPARENTS

Godparents

*Guidelines for Parents
and Godparents*

ANNE WATSON

KINGSWAY PUBLICATIONS
EASTBOURNE

Unless otherwise indicated all
Biblical quotations are from the
Jerusalem Bible copyright © Darton Longman & Todd
and Doubleday & Co Inc. 1966, 1967, 1968

Extracts from the Baptism and Confirmation Services are
reproduced, with permission, from the *Alternative Service
Book* 1980 copyright © The Central Board of Finance of
the Church of England

Front cover and text illustrations by Janet Lunt

British Library Cataloguing in Publication Data

Watson, Anne
  Godparents.
  1. Godparenthood. Christian viewpoints
  I. Title
  261.8'35874

  ISBN 0-86065-646-2

Production and printing in Great Britain for
KINGSWAY PUBLICATIONS LTD
1 St Anne's Road, Eastbourne, E Sussex BN21 3UN by
Nuprint Ltd, 30b Station Road, Harpenden, Herts AL5 4SE

To my godchildren

Sarah, Rachel, Edward, Ruth, Catherine,
Jonathan, Paul, Saskia and Helen,

and my 'adopted' godchildren

Anthony, Damian and Alice.

Contents

Foreword

Like the author of this book, I have many godchildren, and I am painfully conscious of how little I have done for them. We correspond at Christmas and Easter, we meet occasionally, and I try to pray for them regularly, though with diminishing knowledge and understanding as they grow older. It comes as something of a shock to realise that the baby I met at the font is now an undergraduate or even a grandparent.

Anne Watson's book would have been a great help to me all these years—and indeed I still hope to profit from it. There are ideas galore in it which I welcome—and wish I had thought of them myself. She has written a book which is authoritative without being dogmatic, comprehensive without being laboured, positive without being partisan.

I recommend it to new godparents wondering what their obligations are, or old godparents like myself who are conscious of their shortcomings. Thank you, Anne, for an admirable guide to a very important aspect of the Church's ministry.

Stuart Blanch.

The Most Revd & Rt Hon Lord Blanch of Bishopsthorpe

Introduction

I 'inherited' thirteen godchildren when I got married! My husband was a clergyman and therefore an obvious choice for the role of godparent. However, it was not until I had godchildren of my own, and was 'around' when they were growing up, that I discovered the things that I want to share with you in this book.

For many years there have been different views about baptism. Some sections of the church insist baptism is for believing adults only—'believer's baptism'. Others are sure that it is right to baptise babies of believing parents. I am one of those who believe strongly in the rightness of baptising babies and in the institution of godparents.

Even if you do not agree with me, I hope there will be things that will encourage and help you as you seek to bring up children in the household of God. We all need support in this, whether it is from godparents, sponsors, family or friends.

Anne Watson

Part One

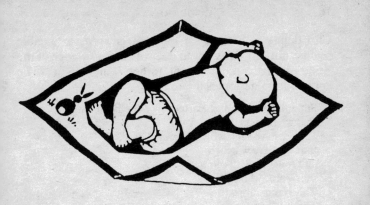

1

Understanding the baptismal vows

Once the initial excitement after the birth of a child has died down the question of baptism arises—if not voiced by the parents themselves then by anxious relatives and friends! An initial visit to the vicar will raise two questions: our own understanding of and commitment to the Christian faith, and the need to choose godparents.

Let's deal with the first question—our understanding of and commitment to the Christian faith. In the baptism service these words are read out: 'Those who bring children to be baptised need to affirm their allegiance to Christ....'

We can do our children a great disservice if we bring them to baptism but are not personally committed to Jesus Christ and his body—the church. Children, especially in their early years, learn by imitating those around them. If we as parents are not revealing God to them by the way we live then they will be retarded as Christians.

15

Christianity is basically a life that is *lived*, a tangible reality, not just an assent to doctrine or knowledge of the Bible. Initially it is 'caught rather than taught'. The apostle John describes it like this:

> Something which has existed since the beginning,
> that we have heard,
> and we have seen with our own eyes;
> that we have watched
> and touched with our hands:
> the Word, who is life—
> This is our subject.
> That life was made visible (1 Jn 1:1–2).

Is Jesus Christ real to us? The Holy Spirit has been sent by God so that we might know the Son of God in a personal way. John and the rest of the disciples knew him first in the flesh but later in the Spirit. He puts it like this:

> What we have seen and heard
> we are telling you
> so that you may be in union with us,
> as we are in union
> with the Father
> and with his Son Jesus Christ (1 Jn 1:3).

As parents and godparents we need to be in union with the Father and with his Son Jesus Christ if we want our children to inherit all the blessings of the kingdom of God. Baptism is God's pledge of this.

In the service parents and godparents will be asked three important questions.

1. Do you turn to Christ?

Turning to Christ means bringing the whole of our lives under the authority of Jesus Christ. He calls us and our children to a new way of living.

Jesus Christ was sent into the world by God to establish a new kingdom. King Herod was very anxious when the three wise men asked him for information about the new king whose star they had seen in the east. He thought this new king might want to take over his kingdom.

However the kingdom of God would have no geographical boundaries. This kingdom would be seen in the lives of those who turned to Christ and followed him. Although it will not be fully established until Jesus returns to claim it. That is why we pray

Our Father in heaven
May your name be held holy
Your kingdom come

There is, however, a barrier that prevents us coming in to the kingdom of God. That barrier is our sin.

In the Old Testament we see that God is utterly holy and man sinful. For sinful man to see God face to face would mean death. Moses asked God if he could see him, he was told to hide in the cleft of a rock. God passed by but Moses only saw his back.

This holy God expected holy living from his people in relation to him and each other. Breaking God's laws was punishable by death, ie the shedding of the blood of the sinner. However God modified this by allowing an animal to be used as a substitute. The animal had to be without a blemish and the one most frequently used was a lamb.

When Jesus came to the Jordan to be baptised, John saw him and prophesied 'Look there is the lamb of God that takes away the sin of the world' (Jn 1:29). When Jesus was sacrificed on the cross our sins could be forgiven because of the shedding of his blood and we were free to enter the kingdom of God.

What *we* have to do is to repent of our sins.

2. Do you repent of your sins?

Repentance is not something we should be afraid of; it is the doorway to freedom.

God's standards cannot be set aside lightly 'since all have sinned and fall short of the glory of God' is the way the Bible describes it (Rom 3:23 RSV). The Ten Commandments in the Old Testament, the teachings of Jesus and the New Testament writers were not given to restrict our freedom but to keep us out of danger. Sadly we have all chosen at one time or another to go our own way and not God's. We find ourselves not living lives that are turned to Christ but to ourselves and material things and even to evil purposes.

For this we need to say sorry to God. This is what it means to repent.

We are not always conscious of our sin but the Holy Spirit can be an honest friend to us—the sort of friend who tells us uncomfortable truths about ourselves. The Bible calls this 'conviction of sin'.

As we prepare for a baptism, whether parents or godparents, we need to ask the Holy Spirit to show us our sins so that we can repent and be forgiven. The promise to us is this

> If we confess our sins, he is faithful and just, and will forgive our sins and cleanse us from all unrighteousness (1 Jn 1:9 RSV).

3. Do you renounce evil?

Our newspapers are full of evidence that our world is riddled with evil. It is important to remember, however, that seriously evil actions and habits often come from small beginnings. What could be more evil than for Judas to betray Jesus for money? The Bible shows us that this evil love of money in Judas started in a small way. In John's gospel we read that Judas used to steal from the common purse of the disciples—and there cannot have been much to steal! (Jn 12:6)

The question of evil has taken on added importance in recent years with the rise of all sorts of occult and related practices. The reading of horoscopes is expressly forbidden in scripture (Jer 27:9) and yet it has become a national pastime—newspapers, magazines, radio and TV and consumer goods all include signs of the zodiac.

Ouija boards and tarot cards are displayed openly for sale in shops and their use is widespread. They are looked upon as harmless games.

Consulting mediums and spiritualists is also condemned by God. They are dangerous practices. Most people seem unaware of the danger they are in and treat the whole business as 'a bit of fun'. But unless we renounce all such evil and turn away from it we can not only find our own lives disturbed and damaged, there can also be harmful effects for our children.

Sometimes we need specific help to free us from these practices or influences. Ministers who take baptism preparation classes will be able to make provision for this.

There are many helpful books and teaching tapes on the market that expand the Christian faith more fully.

2

Choosing godparents

The choice of godparents has been reduced in many instances to a social obligation or a source of expensive presents! One of my husband's godchildren held him in high esteem as he believed him to be the giver of the wonderful presents he received on his birthday and at Christmas-time. It was a case of mistaken identity as it was his other godfather who was able to be so very generous!

There are a number of important things to consider when choosing godparents. It is traditional to have two men and one woman for a boy and two women and one man for a girl. However that is only the legal minimum. When we lived in a household community of eight people, the whole household were godparents to a baby born to a couple who lived with us for six months!

Much more important than the numbers are the 'qualifications' of godparents. As I have written in the previous chapter, faith in Christ is absolutely vital.

I always think it advisable to choose, as one of the godmothers, a woman who has brought up children of her own. Paul in his letter to Titus advises that the 'older women...should show the younger women how they should love their husbands and love their children' (Tit 2:3–4). She will have a wealth of experience behind her which will be of immense help to a new and younger mother.

Many people today are so isolated from their own natural families that bringing up children can be a lonely and frustrating business. If we can allow our children's godparents to help, advise and encourage us we shall benefit enormously. As godmother to a number of children I have made myself available to their parents for advice and help whenever they want it. They have also given me permission to point out things to them which need adjusting and correction. Godfathers too can fulfil such a role, and need to be encouraged to do so.

This does not mean that single people are excluded—they have much to contribute as godparents. By not having direct family commitments of their own they are in fact freer to be involved with the child. An extra pair of hands on a family outing is much appreciated by both parents and godchild alike. Single godparents can well become part of the extended family and be involved very deeply in a way that married godparents cannot. Also, being involved with families with small children is a marvellous training ground not only for marriage, but for keeping people earthed in reality!

If the child's parents are of different nationalities it is helpful to have godparents who represent their dual belonging. This may not be possible, but choosing someone who has a direct interest and knowledge of the country from which one of the parents has come will be a great help. There is so much richness in different cultures which can be easily lost to a child if its godparents are only chosen from the country in which it is living. A brother or sister of the parents, or perhaps a missionary or someone who has lived and worked in the country where one of the parents came from originally are ideas to consider. This can also be really appreciated by the parent who is living away from the homeland and can often feel isolated in a different environment. This does not only apply to children of couples from very different cultures but also to those with a lot in common. One of my godchildren has a Scottish mother and an English father, and a number of people in the congregation to which I belong have Scandinavian and German mothers and English fathers.

If it is at all possible it is wise to make sure that at least one godparent lives nearby. Regular contact with child and parents is vital. A number of my godchildren live far away and I rarely see them, so many of the things described in this book I am unable to do for them.

However I have discovered certain ways to operate as an 'absentee' godmother. I encourage the parents to keep me posted with the child's interests. Is this the time for large Lego bricks or Peter Rabbit books? What television programmes or football clubs are favourites? What is the latest craze at school? Has stamp collecting or any other collecting started? And so on. I then make a point of getting information about all these things so that when birthdays come up I can send something topical. I spent a whole week recently looking at children's TV to find out about Super Ted and others!

I also introduce my godchildren to things I used to enjoy at their age and still do. I send sets of special issue

stamps to one godson regularly and have just introduced another godchild to the fun of stamp collecting by sending him a stamp book and hinges—don't forget the hinges! I now save stamps for him and send a bundle regularly with a letter and my news.

Most children enjoy receiving letters, and if a child is away at boarding school an extra letter is always welcome. When sending a gift I let the child know that there is no need to write a 'thank you letter', otherwise the gift can turn into a burden rather than a joy and godmothers/fathers can become very unpopular. Boys especially hate letter writing.

The gift of a subscription to a conservation society is a good idea for a godchild with an interest in animals or

birds. These organisations send out beautifully illustrated magazines together with information about special exhibitions and holidays, and the magazines come at
regular intervals, which helps to remind the child of the
continuing interest of the godparent.

Children also love growing things, and a packet of
seeds can easily be popped into an envelope. Some of my
older godchildren have been experimenting with growing bonsai trees: there are many inexpensive kits on the
market. I introduced them to this fascinating hobby after
my first visit to the Chelsea flower show.

I pray very specifically that I will be given new and
original ways to build up a relationship with my godchildren even though I only see some of them occasionally. Just recently I sent one of my godsons a tape and
book of *Winnie the Pooh* for his birthday. The idea came
into my head after I had been praying for him. Little did
I know that his parents were giving him a child's tape
recorder as a present and *Winnie the Pooh* was his
favourite story! The Holy Spirit is full of ideas—after all,
he created the world and look at the variety there is in it.

If I am unable to be present at a godchild's confirmation a little while before the service I send them a book
about the Holy Spirit written by my late husband (*Be
Filled With The Spirit* by David Watson). The Confirmation Service speaks a lot about the Holy Spirit and I
think it would help a young person understand the work
of the Holy Spirit. I may also send a book called *My
Faith*[1] to which I contributed a chapter as it includes my
own experiences of being filled with the Spirit. The
shortened form of the video *Jesus Then And Now*[2] could
also be very helpful and comes with a beautifully illustrated book. Many churches use the full form of this
video as preparation for confirmation, so the book that

goes with the series would be a good idea as a present for confirmation itself.

Christian books and videos are a very useful means of encouraging godchildren and parents, and godparents should make good use of them. Of course videos are expensive to buy, but they can be hired by post nowadays.[3] Recently I read an article about a new video of the Old Testament made especially for children by a couple who have produced programmes for television in animated form. I sent the information to the parents of all my godchildren.

As well as giving my godchildren books I often send their parents books as well. James Dobson has written a number of books for parents which are very helpful—*Dare To Discipline* and *Discipline While You Can*[4] give clear understanding and guidelines on discipline. In *Hide and Seek* he shows the importance of affirming a child. Maggie Durran is another writer who works with children and her book *Hello, I'm A Person Too*[5] is excellent.

Praying for healing in the family is the subject and subtitle of a helpful book by Francis MacNutt, *The Prayer That Heals*.[6]

Many marriages are under a great deal of stress and strain at the moment and children suffer because of it. Godparents can provide not only support in prayer but also by sending the parents some of the excellent books on marriage and family life. I have recently sent three to a godchild's parents—*Marriage On The Mend* and *Conflict: Friend or Foe*[7] by Joyce Huggett, and (for fathers) *The Father Heart of God*[8] by Floyd McLung. Sending books helps to fulfil the role I see for godparents of not only being involved with the child but also being resource to the parents as well.

Tapes of talks are also useful and whenever I speak to groups of parents about children and the Christian faith I have the talk taped so I can send it to the parents of my godchildren.[9]

Parents today are often under a great deal of pressure and have little time to hunt for books and tapes or read information about new publications, so godparents can be a great help in this area. Spending time in the local Christian bookshop once a month is one way of finding out what is available. I use some of the money I 'tithe' to buy books for both godchildren and their parents. It is one way, as an absentee godmother I can fulfil the promises I made at the child's baptism.

I have a gallery of pictures of my godchildren in my house. I always ask for a photo, if possible once a year, from the parents of godchildren I see infrequently. I also send the child a photo of me, although not so frequently! It is good for a godparent to have a photograph taken outside the house as this helps the child to see you *in situ*. If you have any special sport you play then a picture of you in action is another way of 'explaining' something about yourself. I walk my dog a lot and someone took a good photo of both of us. So I sent this with a letter to all my godchildren. There was more interest in the dog than in me from what I can gather!

Holidays can be an especially pressurised time for parents with the all too familiar cry from their childlren, 'What shall I do next?' When I am on holiday I pray for inspiration on ideas that will help my godchildren. During a special holiday in Venice, after my husband died, I was visiting St Mark's church which is covered with mosaics of biblical events. At the bookstall I saw a postcard of one of these mosaics depicting Noah in the ark releasing the dove. I bought one each for all my younger godchildren and wrote on it suggesting that they could choose a story from the Bible and illustrate it in mosaic form using coloured paper. Waiting for me when

I returned home were lovely mosaic pictures and grateful letters from the parents. The project had kept their children occupied for the whole of a wet afternoon.

Postcards are an alternative to letters, and I make good use of the wide choice available in a city like York to interest my absent godchildren—the Vikings, the Romans, medieval city walls and houses, and kings who became Christians. After part of the roof of the Minster was damaged by fire there were postcards in abundance and I sent these too. It was national news and to have a postcard from York was quite a triumph for one of my godchildren. Some of my godchildren were very interested to hear that Rowntree Macintosh, the maker of Smarties and Fruit Gums, is based in York. I think they were hoping for some free samples!

I have not used the telephone very much to keep in touch with my godchildren but it can be a useful instrument, more so if your godchild used to live near and has now moved away. I sometimes think it is rather awkward for a child to speak on the phone to a person they meet very occasionally and hardly know. It usually turns into a prompting session from one of the parents! However a 'chat' via a tape might help children to 'know' you in a more relaxed way.

I pray for my godchildren constantly but not just because their names are on a list, in fact I don't keep prayer lists as I always lose them. I ask the Holy Spirit to nudge me often and bring them to my mind. When I see babies being baptised I am reminded about the promises I have made as a godmother and I pray for the children I am responsible for at the same time. I often get new ideas when I do this, and as I do the things I have described in this chapter I pray for the children too.

Keeping in touch with children you do not see often is very important if the role of godparent is going to have

3

Preparing for the baptism service

A godparent's duties start 'officially' at the baptism service, but for many parents I know a helping hand in the preparation beforehand is always welcome. On the day of a baptism relatives and friends gather to celebrate and the child's mother can be under a lot of pressure with extra people staying in the house and sometimes a fairly large number of guests arriving for lunch or tea, depending on the time of the service.

If a godparent is blessed with culinary skills, then offering to help with the catering would probably be appreciated. Perhaps coming to the house before the service to help lay tables and arrange furniture etc would also be welcomed, especially if the baby is being breast-fed. Babies do not always co-operate as far as timing schedules are concerned! They often react to upheaval by refusing to feed or sleep when they are expected to. A godparent on the spot could help to calm a fretful baby and release its mother to attend to any other children and preparations for the celebrations to come. Wearing an apron or overall will protect special outfits. Offering transport for guests or relatives would be appreciated too.

Baptism gifts

It is customary for godparents to give a gift to commemorate the occasion and this can sometimes pose quite a problem. Recently I heard a prospective godmother discussing the merits of different presentation Bibles in a local bookshop. The contents did not seem to be important, just the size and binding! A King James' Authorised Version of the Bible with a white leather cover is going to be of little practical use to a child even when it can read. All it will become is a sentimental memento. If you want to give the child a Bible then one with lots of pictures, preferably coloured and in a modern text is a much better idea. This can be upgraded at birthdays as the child grows older.

I tend to give my godchildren a Bible when they are at the stage of being interested in books. For a baptismal present I give them a candle (usually white) and a suitable holder to put it in. Many ministers present candles to parents and godparents on behalf of the child at baptism with these words:

> Receive this light.
> This is to show that you have passed
> from darkness to light.
> Shine as a light in the world
> to the glory of God the Father.

For godchildren who are girls I choose a floral china holder or a pretty one in pottery; for boys often a pottery or metal one with a modern design. I enclose a little card and quote the last two lines of the minister's words. These holders are never out of date even when a child has grown up. A matching one could be given at Confirmation or a special birthday to form a pair. They are also essential for the annual Advent candle, but more of that later.

A more expensive idea is a napkin ring in silver or other material with the child's initials engraved on it. This is a present that will have a long term use. Silver or stainless steel mugs are popular presents too, as are adjustable bangles for little girls. A pusher and spoon set is another possibility, although this form of cutlery is not so popular today.

Sometimes family jewellery is passed on by godmothers who are relatives, and investments of money—especially by godfathers—are often made as well. Some godparents open Savings Accounts and add to them at birthdays and at Christmas, only giving the child a token present at those times. These savings will eventually accumulate and be a very welcome asset to a child when it is older.

Some godparents prefer to give the child a gift of clothing like a beautiful shawl to wrap it in during the ceremony—a very welcome present in some large and cold Anglican churches! Those who have sewing gifts might like to make a special gown for the baby, which could become an heirloom if there is not one in the family already, or perhaps a beautifully smocked dress or romper suit for a child who is slightly older.

Preparation classes

Most ministers hold baptism preparation classes which help parents to understand the significance of the step they are taking. I think that prospective godparents should attend these classes too if this is at all possible. After all they will be making the same promises on behalf of the child as are the parents.

A baby in church

Bringing a child to baptism can be quite a nerve-racking business; especially if the baptism takes place during a church service. Many people are very relaxed just sitting in a pew on Sunday but become a bundle of nerves at the thought of being singled out for special attention. In our church in York we have a mobile font which is placed on a fairly high stage during the Family Service so that the whole congregation can see what is going on.

If the baptism service is the first time a couple have been in church since their wedding they can feel extremely nervous. Babies are so unpredictable and can cause embarrassment so easily by yelling lustily or filling their nappies just as they are handed to the minister. If church-going has not been a regular habit then choosing a godmother who does go to church and is comfortable in such surroundings would be wise.

Get familiar with the surroundings

If the family are new to the area it might well be advisable to attend a service on a number of Sundays before the baptism takes place. Children as well as adults benefit from becoming familiar with new surroundings. The unfamiliar noise of the organ can make some babies cry, and being confined to a pew can be difficult when there are toddlers in the family. It is much better to get some of these difficulties ironed out before the big day. Pro-

spective godparents who live near could also be invited
so that they too can be more relaxed on the day of the
baptism.

Some churches have a Family Service every Sunday
morning, but there are others who worship together
once a month. The times of services are usually to be
found on the notice-board outside the church. If not,
then a phone call to the church secretary or vicar will
supply the information. Alternatively, if you know a
family who already attends the church regularly you
could ask them if they will take you and show you the
ropes. Not only how to find your way through the service
book, but where to park the baby buggy or pram, where
the loo and creche are situated, and so on. It is not such
an ordeal in a totally new situation if there is someone
with you who is familiar with the proceedings. Godparents who are members of the church could also fulfil
this role and perhaps come prepared with a Sunday bag
for smaller children if necessary (see page 37).

One other helpful thing to do for children if the service is a Parish Eucharist (Communion), is to give them
the illustrated version of the *Rite A Holy Communion
Service*. It is called *The Lord is Here*[1]. It is small enough
for little hands to hold, as well as sitting comfortably on
the pew ledge. Some of the larger versions for children
are liable to be knocked off small ledges and cause a
commotion. *The Lord is Here* has coloured illustrations
on each page and the text clearly printed for those who
can read. Pointing out to the child the link between what
is happening in the service and the illustrations in the
book keeps a child's attention from wandering. It is a
good idea to give the child the book a day or two before
the service, explaining the pictures and so exciting the
child's imagination and expectation, so that Sunday will

be an experience to look forward to. It will also help any parents who are new to a Parish Eucharist.

I have given this little book to all my godchildren as soon as they are past the paper eating stage! Holding your own book in church can make you feel very important. It doesn't matter at all if it is grasped firmly upside down, as one of my charges used to do! Once a month we have a Family Communion instead of the usual Family Service and we have encouraged all parents to buy this book for their children. One Sunday I noticed a number of children round me were holding up their books to each other to show that they had found the right place and that they had a copy. This helped some children to feel really part of the church—the body of Christ.

The whole family at the baptism service

The corporate nature of the church is expressed clearly in the opening prayer of the baptism service where the congregation asks God to:

> receive this child *into the Family of the Church*;
> that he/she *may walk with us* in the way of Christ
> and grow in the knowledge of your love.

This is further emphasised towards the end of the service when the congregation says these words:

> We welcome you into the Lord's Family.
> We are members together of the Body of Christ,
> we are children of the same Heavenly Father;
> we are inheritors together of the Kingdom of God.
>   We welcome you.

Unless there are very special circumstances it is much better for children to be baptised in the context of the whole church gathered together for worship. Parents and children need the help and encouragement of other Christians constantly if they are going to enjoy all the benefits of the life of Jesus, and grow to be like him and eventually be received into his heavenly kingdom.

Although some parents are nervous about a church service and would possibly prefer a private baptism on a Sunday afternoon, the whole point of what they and the godparents are committing themselves and the child to is undermined. Christian baptism is not just for the child, its godparents and the rest of the family. It should be a public declaration in the presence of the church when it is gathered for worship. The church can then accept its full responsibility to support and help the whole family to be faithful to the promises that have been made.

It is not only babies that can be unpredictable at important moments, their older brothers and sisters can be too. I have witnessed some very distraught parents during baptism services with little children who will not obey their injunctions and persist in running amok. If children are not taught to respond to discipline at home then there is no likelihood of them doing so in a public place. They are also more likely to misbehave if attention is being focused on a new baby.

There are a number of things that can be done to try and prevent this happening. If the child is old enough then a simple explanation in advance of what will be happening in church will help, especially if this is accompanied with stories of the child's own baptism. If there are photos of the occasion then get them out and show the child. Acting out the service with a doll as a substitute for the baby is also entertaining. It may even be necessary to resort to bribery! Promising the child a special treat if they behave (specify how!) during the baptism. Always allow the small child to take a favourite toy or blanket to the church. Being able to cuddle this will be a great comfort to the child when he, or she, is feeling insecure and self-conscious. So many parents leave these sort of things at home because they are worn and tatty.

It is wise to decide in advance who will be in charge of a toddler while the baby is being baptised as it is very distracting for everyone if a child is being passed from one person to the next. If necessary invite the child's favourite adult friend to help you—either a relative or its own grandmother.

This is not to say that a child has to stand stock-still. There is no reason why a small child cannot move closer for a better look at the proceedings. I have seen children stand really close to the font watching and listening only to have an embarrassed and over-anxious parent come and lift them away. This has resulted in opposition from the children and commotion all round while everyone tries to sort things out.

If a child really does get to the point of no return then he, or she, should be removed to the creche or out of ear shot. It is always wise to find out where the exits are in a church, especially the one nearest the font.

Knowing where the loos are will save time and avoid unhappy accidents. It is a good idea to ask the minister to show you round the church if it is a building you are not familiar with. This facility is given to people getting married so why not for those with children coming to be baptised?

It is traditional for a godmother to hold the baby and pass it to the minister, or receive the child from the minister. A word of warning to all godmothers at this point—once babies can sit up by themselves they are very curious about things that hang round peoples' necks or from their ears. I would always avoid wearing neck-laces or earrings that dangle down. They are liable to come in for some rough treatment. Brooches too are another attraction, and hats with feathers that curl over the front of the brim. Large brimmed hats in general are very tempting to a slightly older baby. It is also advisable to have a good-sized handkerchief or tissue in a pocket as babies have a tendency to dribble, or worse! Get a little practice, too, in holding the baby before the day. It not only helps a godparent to feel more competent but few babies feel sure in the arms of a total stranger.

Toddlers cannot be expected to sit still through the baptism of a baby brother or sister. A small bag with some carefully chosen toys will keep a child happily occupied without disrupting the service for everyone else. There are many attractive children's bags on the market: some made out of PVC with Peter Rabbit and other favourite nursery stories as decoration. Thomas the Tank Engine is also well represented. I like making patchwork and have sewn 'Sunday bags' for all my god-daughters. These colourful bags are filled with special toys, books and so on that the child can play with quietly during a church service. The contents can be changed regularly to make sure the Sunday bag is a source of enjoyment and interest.

After children leave the nursery-school age I tend to replace the contents of the bags with something more appropriate—with drawing equipment, paper pads, rulers, pencils, pens and so on. Plastic carrier bags are not a good idea as they are rather large and they rustle when little people are trying to find something in them.

For the baptism service a book with pictures about baptisms would help to focus a child's attention on what is happening. Perhaps one depicting Jesus' baptism. Pencils and a drawing pad will keep little fingers busy. It is better to avoid felt-tip pens as the ink can mark clothing and church books—also a pad is better than loose sheets of paper. Rescuing a precious drawing that has floated under the pew in front can cause a major upheaval!

Toys that make a noise should definitely be banned. They will be used to attract attention at all the wrong moments. Hide them the night before the service then there is less likely to be a battle just before going to church. A gift of a doll to a little girl, especially a 'baby' doll is a good idea. It can then be brought to church and 'looked after' during the service—perhaps even be baptised when it gets home. Children often like to act out events they have seen. Something special for a little boy is necessary too. New babies get a lot of attention and presents, and having something special saved for the day of the baptism helps other brothers and sisters not to feel left out. It also helps to occupy their attention when concentration is wandering in the service. I give my godchildren a small present for the church service when their baby brothers or sisters are being baptised and offer to sit with the family if there is room in the pew, and certainly nearby so that I can be on hand to help— taking them to the loo or explaining what is going on.

Godparents can be a great help with practical preparations for the actual baptism service—thus ensuring it will be a day to remember for all the right reasons!

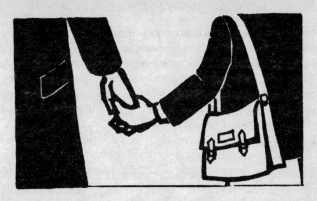

4

Keeping in touch with growing godchildren

It is only since I have been godmother to some children in York, where I live, that I have begun to develop a fuller understanding of the role of godparent.

Being able to visit my 'charges' and worship with them and their families in our Family Service each Sunday morning has helped a strong bond to grow. I even ministered to these children and their mothers before they were born! During the time of the Peace at Holy Communion I would put my arms round the mother and lay my hand on her abdomen and say 'Peace be with *both of you*.' Similarly when giving out the wine or the bread (I am an elder in the church and commissioned to do so by the local bishop) I would always say 'The body/blood of Christ keep *both of you* in eternal life.' If twins or more babies are expected then 'all of you' would be more appropriate!

At house groups and other meetings I always pray with and lay hands on those who are pregnant. Normally godparents are chosen after the baby is born, but if I know I am to be a godmother before the child is born then I ask the parents to let me know immediately labour starts so that I can begin to pray. I usually do not want to be rung in the middle of the night unless there are known complications.

As mentioned earlier, it is most advisable to choose at least one godparent who can have regular contact with the child and its family. This contact should start as soon as the choice of godparents is made. Those who are chosen should be able to start getting to know their godchild as soon as possible. It is perhaps easier for godmothers as babies are more likely to appeal to them, but in this enlightened age I am certainly not ruling out the men! If a baby, especially a boy, is separated from its own father through death, divorce or the fact that its mother is not married, then it is important for the god-father to get to know the child as early as possible. This would probably be made much easier if two of the god-parents were a married couple.

The parents of my godchildren have been marvellous in allowing me to hold their little sons and daughters as often as possible. I have often taken them to the Com-munion rail in my arms, as well as rocked them to sleep so that their mother can finish cooking the lunch. I also make myself available to pray for them if they are sick.

Baby sitting is a service that godparents can give as well, and having a regular sitter is a boon to parents and security for the child.

When my children were young the baby buggy had not been invented, so it has taken me a while to become competent in its use. While visiting a godchild recently I was introduced to the advisability of having swivel wheels that could lock; I think it is less complicated to drive a car! Whenever any of my godchildren are put in a buggy the first thing I do is go out and buy them a sunshade. The clear plastic covers that are made are useless in protecting a child from the glare of the sky, even in winter. I see so many small babies trying desperately to avoid the bright light they are subjected to each time they are taken out. If only the manufacturers would spend five minutes looking up at the sky they would soon make the hoods and rain shields in an anti-glare material.

I always try to mark different stages in my godchildren's development with some sort of helpful recognition and encouragement. When they are going to be weaned I give their mothers a horn teaspoon. Babies can so easily reject their first solids when a cold metal object like an ordinary teaspoon is put into their mouths. Weaning can be an anxious time, especially for a first-time mother and a godmother's advice and help can make all the difference.

Godmothers who have brought up children of their own can provide support and advice for anxious parents during times of teething, infectious illnesses, and so on. Being available to the parents of godchildren for counselling and advice, if they would like it, is a valuable service older godparents can offer.

One godparent I know likes to help with buying new shoes for her godchildren, or any other special expense that might be a real burden for the parents. When a child is starting school or changing schools, help with the new school uniform could be given. The first pair of ballet shoes or football boots, or some games equipment might be other welcome gifts. It is not only a matter of helping with the expenses but being involved at important milestones in a godchild's life.

Starting school is a major event in a child's life and as a godparent I have been involved with some of my godchildren's parents in helping them to choose a school, and linking them up with other families whose children are already at the school. The Christian faith is under attack in quite a number of our schools and careful investigation and prayer is vital before committing a child to a specific school. In some areas choice is limited or non-existent, so godparents need to be aware of the facts so they can pray effectively as well as support both the child and its parents practically. A godparent who is or has been a teacher would be a great help in many ways as the child goes through school.

I encourage my godchildren to talk to me about going to school. I try and find out what they are looking forward to and what is difficult or fearful for them. I always give them a 'going to school' present and send them a postcard with a suitable picture. The Medici Society has some lovely Margaret Tarrant reproductions (eg *Woodland School*). Another idea is to draw a picture yourself—you can always copy something from a book if your artistic abilities are minimal. I copied a picture of Jewish boys being taught by a Rabbi in the time of Jesus and sent it to my godson before his first day at school, with a letter to say that this was the sort of school Jesus would have gone to. I wanted to remind him that Jesus went to school too, and plant in his mind the fact that God is involved in all our experiences of growing up. This helps to show that God is a present reality rather than a Sunday-only person. There are quite a number of helpful books, too, that explain what goes on in a school for those joining the reception and infant classes.

If you have a car then helping to chauffeur children to school can provide time for asking questions and can often reveal areas of difficulty or delight. Walking to school with them helps in the same way. What is gleaned from these times provides fuel for prayer as well as ideas for birthday presents, and hard-pressed parents will bless you for your help.

Perhaps a little research in a local library could reveal some choice piece of information that could be given to a child to help with his studies or classroom projects.

Godparents can also be a great help during Sunday worship. I am able to be in church quite early on Sunday mornings so can save a seat beside me for my godchild, his younger brother, baby sister and mother. His father has to be in church early too as he is the Musical Director and is needed to supervise the Children's Orchestra practice as well as the choir. Having a seat reserved means that the mother does not have to leave home too early or worry about finding a seat when she does get there—no easy thing with a baby and two active small boys! She can arrive just before the service begins.

This would apply too if you are godparents to a vicar's child. I remember struggling to get my children to church by myself each week as my husband had to leave early to check on all the arrangements for the service. The phone never stopped ringing and one of the children always seemed to have fallen over and cut something just when we were about to leave!

Sitting with your godchild is also a good idea as you can experience worshipping together. You can also provide an extra knee and a listening ear, or a safe means of getting to the loo—especially if the mother is tied up with a new brother or sister. It can also work the other way round. I sometimes hold the baby brother or sister while my godchild can have some uninterrupted time with his mother through the service. Godparents can provide an invaluable service and help to make Sunday worship an enjoyable and learning experience for the whole family.

If your godchild attends Sunday school rather than a Family Service then a godparent who is a Sunday school teacher or helper has many advantages. In addition to the Family Service on Sundays we run what we call a 'Children's Workshop'. This is held early on a Friday evening and is for children between five and eleven years old. The whole aim of this worship is to help children to relate lovingly together and out of that relationship serve the church on Sunday with dance or mime, making special banners and Communion bread, and so on. They are also taught how to listen and respond to the Holy Spirit during the week, read the Scriptures and share together what they have heard from God. I encourage the godparents at our church to get involved with this workshop so they and their godchildren can learn together to be brothers and sisters in Christ and serve his body, the church.

When children enter the teenage years they tend to communicate with friends of their own age, but if godparents have built up a good relationship with them through their earlier years they can provide helpful adult input. This is very valuable when parents' ideals and beliefs are being rejected or questioned. It may well be that some godparents are involved in the youth work of their church, and they can then share in this aspect of their godchildren's lives. Teenagers are often more likely to confide in their youth leaders than in their parents at certain stages. This presupposes that as a godchild is growing up the godparent has become his confidante as well as that of his parents.

This is the time too when the question of Confirmation arises. Godparents should encourage their godchildren to think seriously about their own commitment to the Christian faith and help them to prepare to make the promises for themselves, that were made on their behalf at baptism.

This is a good time to give a teenage godchild a new and more up to date version of the Bible if theirs is old, together with a subscription for a supply of suitable Bible-study notes. These can be obtained from a Christian bookshop or through the church bookstall. Without the incentive of study notes most Bibles are left on the shelf. A Bible is not a text book or reference book but a manual for life. When a young adult hears God speaking through the pages of Scripture and responds, then he is on the way to becoming a fully mature person.

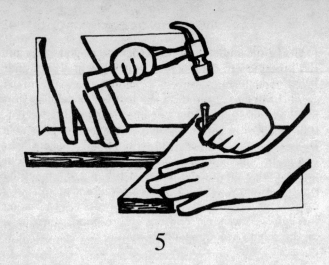

5

Godfathers and godchildren

Godmothers seem to play a much larger part in the lives
of their godchildren than godfathers—perhaps because
they are more adept in the early years than most men.
However, economic situations today have reversed the
role of homemaker for some families and men find they
are rapidly gaining skills in child care.

But this situation is still the exception to the rule and
godfathers need to be encouraged to see that there are
more ways to fulfil their obligations than sending presents at appropriate times. Married godfathers usually
have their wives to prod them into action, whereas single
men are often at a loss for ideas.

One of the easiest ways for godfathers to be involved
with their godchildren is natural social interaction. It is
ideal if the godfather has a family of roughly the same
age group, and the two families can get together fairly
often for meals or leisure activities of some sort.

Going on joint family walks is a very good way for godfathers to get to know their godchildren. A godfather could even be encouraged to shoulder a baby in its carrier! Giving a helping hand to a small godchild on rough stretches, pointing out interesting sights, or collecting leaves or other flora for identification later, are ways he can show his care for the child. A small child appreciates a godfather who takes empty match boxes in his pocket for all those creepy crawlies that children love to collect; or a fishing net if you know you will pass near water.

The excellent series of 'I Spy'[1] books are something to produce for a godchild, gathering the information together to complete the book. Kite flying can provide hours of fun for child and adult.

Godchildren appreciate being 'special', and by that I mean being chosen out of their own families to join their godparent's family for the day or for an outing. Pressure from other children in the godchild's family to join in too should be resisted unless the child cannot cope without a brother or sister. The event is made more significant if the godfather can call to collect the godchild in advance rather than arrive at the door with all the rest of his family.

The telephone may, at times, be the only way a godfather can keep in touch. Just a call to say 'hello' will help build the link between godchild and godfather, although it would become a much more exciting event if the phone call was to say that a present was on the way! The child could send its 'thank you's' back by phone too if writing letters proved to be a major obstacle. Receiving a phone call before an important exam or driving test is very encouraging, or an enquiry as to progress at a new sport or activity helps to boost confidence and encourage application if interest is flagging. A godfather with a telephone in his car could make a phone call something worth telling friends about at school!

Another technical way of communication is by tape. It is great fun to play back a message from your own godfather and then perhaps send him one in return. If a godfather plays an instrument or can make special sound effects (eg bird songs or animal impressions!) these could be recorded for a godchild. Children enjoy having a godfather who can do something different—they can bask in reflected glory!

One of my son's godfathers sent him a photograph of the place in which he worked. Admittedly it was a very impressive building—the Guardian Royal Exchange in London—and whenever my son saw a picture of the building he would tell his friends 'that's where my godfather works'. Godfathers who are at college or university could do the same, or even some special landmark in the locality could be used if your godchild lives in a different part of the country.

If a godfather lives in a town that has some special historical interest then he could find out when his godchild would be studying that period at school and send appropriate pictures and information, or even invite the child to stay in order to see things first hand. My godson benefited from postcards and a visit to York when he was studying the Vikings and the Romans for his history lessons.

Many men have to travel abroad in connection with their work. Postcards from foreign places are well received by children, even a picture of a plane in flight—readily available in airport shops. Keeping a supply of such cards in a briefcase is a good reminder.

Some extra tuition in bowling or batting would be something a cricketing godfather could offer a grandson, and a visit together to a Test Match would be very exciting. Going out together for a day's fishing is another idea, although godfathers need to adjust the time spent sitting on the bank to suit the age of the child. Whatever sporting activity godfathers are interested in, they can involve their godchildren too, helping to open up new interests and increase skills.

Fathers will, of course, get lots of ideas from their own children and can pass these on to their godchildren. Being aware of the latest crazes at school, knowing who is currently 'top of the pops', or the finer details of the newest car to be produced, will enable a godfather to talk knowledgeably with a godson on matters that interest him.

Godfathers are especially helpful for godchildren who do not have a father of their own, and prayer and support would be appreciated at anxious times like exams, or decisions about future schooling. An available 'listening ear' outside the immediate family can help to get things into perspective for child and parent alike.

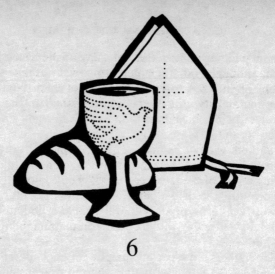

6

Confirmation

The promises made by godparents at baptism need to be ratified by the children themselves at a special service called Confirmation. A bishop presides and this is usually the candidates' first introduction to active participation in the Holy Communion.

I try to be present at my godchildren's Confirmations although this has not always been possible, especially for those of my godchildren who live in other parts of the country.

Children and Holy Communion

There has been considerable debate in the Church about linking Confirmation with Holy Communion. Many people feel that children should be allowed to take the bread and wine as soon as they are able. Through their parents and godparents children have made a commitment to Christ at their baptism, when they were welcomed into the church, the body of Christ. As the congregation says in the conclusion of the baptism service:

We welcome you into the Lord's Family
We are members together of the Body of Christ,

and as members they should be allowed to enjoy all the privileges and blessings that go with membership.

At one stage many children in our church were puzzled that they could not take the bread and wine at Family Communion. We had taught them a lot about being members together with us of the body of Christ. They began to complain, so we took the matter up with our local bishop. He lowered the age for Confirmation, which opened the way for many more children to receive at Communion.

However I have noticed recently in our church that many parents give their children some of their bread and the children take it eagerly. I now make sure I give parents an extra large piece of bread if they have children with them. Of course this is not so easy if wafers are used, but not impossible.

Unconfirmed children still do not take the wine but I always let them look into the cup and tell them that it is very special and one day 'when they are confirmed' they will be able to have some too. This creates a sense of expectancy and acknowledges the present ruling of the Church.

Preparing for Confirmation

Children and adults who are to be confirmed are required to attend a series of classes where they are taught the basis of the Christian faith so that they understand what is involved in their commitment. Godparents can help too by being available to answer questions or discuss a particular subject. If the Confirmation candidates are studying special notes or a particular book on Confirmation it would be wise to try and get a copy. You may well be able to tell godchildren some of your own experiences. Alternatively, there are many books available with accounts of Christians who have committed themselves to following Christ whole-heartedly. These may be particularly helpful to some young people who are confirmed as a matter of course or under pressure because of social convention.

The Bishop's words

In the Confirmation Service the candidates reaffirm the vows made on their behalf as children, and then they kneel before the bishop who stretches his hands towards them and prays:

> Almighty and everliving God,
> you have given your servants new birth
> in baptism by water and the Spirit,
> and forgiven them all their sins.
> Let your Holy Spirit rest upon them:
> the Spirit of wisdom and understanding,
> the Spirit of counsel and inward strength;
> the Spirit of knowledge and true godliness;
> and let their delight be in the fear of the Lord.
> Amen.

Then he lays his hands on their heads and says:

> Confirm, O Lord, your servant...(candidate's name)
> with your Holy Spirit.

What the Bible tells us about the Holy Spirit

The Holy Spirit was promised to the first disciples by Jesus on the eve of his arrest and subsequent death. Jesus knew he was not going to be with them in person for much longer but that his heavenly Father would send his Holy Spirit to be with them for ever:

> I shall ask the Father,
> and he will give you another Advocate
> to be with you for ever,
> that Spirit of truth... (Jn 14:16)

After Jesus rose from the dead he spent forty days with his disciples telling them about the kingdom of God and 'When he had been at table with them, he told them not to leave Jerusalem, but to wait there for what the Father had promised. "It is" he had said "what you have heard me speak about: John baptised with water but you, not many days from now, will be baptised with the Holy Spirit."' (Acts 1:4–5).

He also told them that they would receive power when the Holy Spirit came upon them and they would be his witnesses not only in Jerusalem but through Judea and Samaria and to the ends of the earth (Acts 1:8).

The disciples were obedient and it was on the Day of Pentecost that they were baptised with the Holy Spirit as Jesus had promised. They were initiated into a realm of the supernatural that they had not experienced before. The outcome of which was that a great crowd gathered, and Peter spoke to them about Jesus and urged them to repent of their sins and be baptised, and that they too would receive the gift of the Holy Spirit (Acts 2:38). Three thousand people responded. The power that the Holy Spirit brought had certainly made Peter an effective witness!

We also read in Acts 19:6–7 that Paul laid his hands on twelve men who had been baptised in the name of Jesus and they received the Holy Spirit. This is a helpful example for godchildren who are curious or anxious about the laying on of hands by the bishop. Not all incidences of the coming of the Holy Spirit are pre-ceeded by someone laying hands on another person. One of my godchildren was quite anxious about going up to the bishop and letting him lay his hands on her head. 'Why couldn't the Holy Spirit just come without all that?' she wanted to know!

The Acts of the Apostles goes on to record how many other people and communities responded to those who preached the Good News about Jesus and the signs and wonders that the Holy Spirit effected through them to authenticate the message.

The Holy Spirit in our lives (and our godchildren's lives) today

Our children/godchildren will need to be equipped with the power of the Holy Spirit too if they are to be effective witnesses for Christ. That will depend to a large degree on our own experience and understanding of the work of the Holy Spirit.

It would be wise for godparents to share their own understanding and experiences of the work of the Holy Spirit with the parents of their godchildren, respecting the parents point of view if opinions differ. If I am unable to see my godchildren's parents, then I send them two books and a booklet: *My Faith*[1] to which I contributed a chapter which describes my own encounter with the power of God through the Holy Spirit; *One In The Spirit*[2], and also *Be Filled With The Spirit*[3], both written by my late husband David Watson. They can then give them to my godchild if they agree with the contents.

Godchildren need to be encouraged not only to know the power of the Holy Spirit in their lives and the gifts he brings, but they also need to be taught what the Bible calls 'the fruit of the Spirit': love, joy, peace, patience, kindness, goodness, trustfulness, gentleness and self-control (Gal 5:22–23).

The Holy Spirit also helps us when we get into difficulty in praying. 'The Spirit helps us with our daily problems and in our praying. For we don't even know what we should pray for, nor how to pray as we should: but the Holy Spirit prays for us with such feeling that it cannot be expressed in words.' (Rom 8:26–27 Phillips)

The promise of the Holy Spirit was made for 'you and your children' Peter records in Acts 2:39. What a joy it is to be involved in the preparation of a godchild for such a gift.

Confirmation gifts

It is traditional to give one's godchild a Confirmation present. Girls are often given a cross as a piece of jewellery to hang around their necks; a constant reminder of their commitment to Christ and his love for them. Boys are sometimes given a pen with their name engraved on it, or if they are older, a pair of cuff links suitably engraved.

The books and videos I have already mentioned in Chapter 2 make suitable gifts, or a subscription to a monthly magazine could also be given.

Gathering together verses from the Bible that record the work of the Holy Spirit and writing them in a nicely bound blank page book is something for a godparent to consider, especially if they have gifts in calligraphy.

There is also the possibility of paying for your godchild to go to a special Christian event, or invite them to join with you and your family if you are attending an event in the year of his or her Confirmation. Many young people find it of great help and are challenged through the Greenbelt Festivals[4] and others like them. There are Christian organisations who take young people abroad during the holidays and help them to tell local people about their faith. Horizons[5] enable older children to spend time in France. CYFA-Pathfinder Ventures[6] and Crusaders[7] are Christian organisations who run holidays and activities for young people every year.

Once a child has been confirmed many godparents feel their job is done. However children and young adults do need people outside their immediate family to talk to. Perhaps even more so after they have made their own commitment to 'take up their cross' and follow the Lord. Parents, too, can still benefit from sharing their anxieties with those who have a genuine concern and interest in their growing children. Continuing contact with godchildren is very worthwhile.

Church Festivals are times of celebration, when the church family gathers together to commemorate a particular event in the Christian year.

At Christmas most churches are packed as everyone gathers to celebrate the birth of Jesus. On Easter Day Christians rejoice that Christ overcame death and made it possible for us, as believers, to be able to join him in his kingdom. Around these two great festivals other special days are of particular interest to children. The Advent season, with Advent candles and calendars becoming more and more popular each year, is the time of preparation for the event of Christmas. Good Friday and Whitsun have escaped commercialisation but are times to be remembered by regular worshippers. Mothering Sunday and Harvest are both festivals that are popular with adults and children alike.

It is a good idea, if at all possible, to take your godchild to church on these special occasions—or if the whole family already attend these services you could arrange to join them in church.

As godparents you will be expected to know everything about the church, and this section will, I hope, give you enough information and background on the various festivals to enable you to answer any questions your godchildren may ask!

7

Christmas

Background

The early Christians often 'took over' festivals from their own culture and tradition and Christianised them. Roman emperors used to celebrate *Natalis Invicti*—the birth of the Unconquerable One—on the 25th December. The Unconquerable One was the sun—which after the shortest day and longest night began again to give more light to the world. The Christian understanding that Jesus was the Light of the World (Jn 8:12) and the Sun of Righteousness (Mal 4:2) gave the festival a whole new meaning. During this festival the Romans used to decorate their houses with evergreens, and the poor and needy, together with the children, received presents. Early Christians capitalised on the pagan festivals as much as possible.

Advent

Advent is the time in the church's calendar when preparation is made for the coming celebration of the birth of Jesus Christ. Advent also looks forward to his second coming, when he will usher in a new heaven and a new earth.

I mentioned in an earlier chapter my custom in Advent of sending a candle to my godchildren which they can put in the candle holder I gave them when they were baptised. These special candles are marked off in sections and can be enjoyed by the whole family if they are lit during a mealtime. If the child is old enough then he or she could have the honour of lighting it each time (a taper will save burnt fingers and lots of matches!). If the child is too young for this then he, or she, should be allowed to blow it out when the marked area for that day has been reached.

Advent calendars are an alternative. For my older and grown up godchildren who still like a calendar I have found that the Bible Lands Society[1] produce a lovely one each year with a map of Palestine as it was at the time of Jesus, and a suitable episode from the Christmas account behind each 'window'.

There are also excellent activity books for children that give ideas for making cards and presents. I give these to my godchildren in Advent, and they help to give the mounting excitement a practical outlet! Cards with outline drawings for children to colour in and send to their friends can be bought and last year I found inexpensive books that had cut-outs to colour and make into a nativity scene.

Christmas

This is the most exciting festival of the year for children and they seem to be so inundated with presents that it is not always easy to know what to buy for them that is special.

I really enjoy watching my godchildren performing in their school nativity plays. If, for instance, they are playing the part of a shepherd I try and find a small book that tells of the shepherds' involvement in the birth of Christ and give it as a 'bouquet' for their performance. If you can draw, then a picture depicting their part for them to colour in would also be a good idea.

A relatively inexpensive idea is to record the Christmas story on tape yourself in the version of the Bible the child already owns. If you can sing, then record some of the carols or other traditional Christmas songs, giving a short explanation before each one of its origin or anything interesting you can find out about it. (Decorate the tape box with attractive Christmas designs to make it look special otherwise it can seem very uninteresting to a small child and be relegated to the bottom of the toy box!)

If your godchild is the first in a family then something for the Christmas tree, a little wooden angel for instance, which could possibly be the start of a collection for the time when the child is setting up its own home. Thrifty godparents can find such gifts at the January sales at marvellously reduced prices!

Some godparents I know give a very small present and then take their godchild on a special outing—the pantomime, ballet or cinema seem to be favourite choices. Board or card games help children to do things together and with their parents—something to be encouraged in an age where individualism and isolation start early.

The Holy Spirit, who was responsible for the first Christmas, can make us creative in lots of new ways so that our godchildren and their parents experience a fresh touch of the love of God through our giving.

One or two Christian parents have asked me how wise it is to allow their children to believe in the 'myth' of Santa Claus, fearing that when a child realises that Santa is not a real person he or she will think that Jesus is a myth too.

I have not found any children who have dismissed the truth of Christmas when they found out that Santa Claus is a tradition rather than a truth. One way to help a child make the transition from 'make believe' to reality is to explain the origin of Santa Claus.

Santa Claus is a American corruption of the Dutch 'San Nicolaas' (St Nicholas). Dutch settlers introduced the custom to the New World. Not a lot is known about this saint, but he probably lived in the early fourth century AD and was Bishop of Myra. He was imprisoned and tortured during the reign of the Roman Emperor Diocletian, but was released when Constantine became Emperor.

Legend has it that one night he secretly deposited gifts of money at the home of a poor citizen whose three daughters had no hope of getting married without dowries. This was the origin of giving gifts in secret. In some countries the custom is still observed on 5th December, the eve of St Nicholas' Day, but in others it has been transferred to Christmas Eve.

St Nicholas is the patron saint of Russia and the special protector of children, scholars, merchants and sailors. He is often depicted with three children standing at his side. According to legend Nicholas restored three children to life who had been murdered and hidden in a large salting tub.

Epiphany

The coming of the wise men is often included in the Christmas festivities, but many churches still wait to celebrate Epiphany on the third Sunday after Christmas. I like this tradition as Christmas can be over so quickly. I buy Christmas cards depicting the wise men either following the star or presenting their gifts of gold, frankincense and myrrh to the Christ child, and send or give them to my godchildren at Epiphany. One year I asked a very good singer in the congregation to record the carol 'We Three Kings' and gave a copy to each child. If a child can play a musical instrument then the sheet music for this carol could be an alternative.

8

Easter

The next great festival of the Church's year is Easter. The word 'Easter' comes from the Anglo-Saxon *Eostre*—a Saxon deity who was goddess of the Dawn. The pagan festival celebrated the rising of new growth in springtime after the death of winter. With the obvious connections Christians were able to use the festival to celebrate the resurrection of Christ from the dead.

Easter is not celebrated on the same Sunday each year. In the 1662 prayer book the instructions were that Easter Day is the first Sunday after the full moon, which happens on or after the 21st March. If the full moon falls on a Sunday then Easter Day is the following Sunday.

Like Christmas, Easter is preceded by a time of preparation which is called Lent. Just before Lent begins there is the season of Shrovetide. The word 'shrove' is the past tense of the verb 'to shrive', which means 'to confess sins'. People went to church on Shrove Tuesday

66

to be shriven—to confess their sins and receive forgiveness in preparation for the coming of Lent, which began the following day—Ash Wednesday. The whole festival used to last four days beginning on Shrove Saturday, over Shrove Sunday (Quinquagesima), Collop Monday and ending on Shrove Tuesday, or Pancake Day. It was regarded as a holiday for feasting and having fun before the six weeks of the Lenten Fast. During Lent people were forbidden to eat eggs, butter and other fats, meat and all rich foods. These had to be eaten during Shrovetide so that only the bare necessities were left in the larders.

Collop Monday probably got its name from the Norse word meaning 'a slice of meat'. In the North of England people cooked collops on this day—this was bacon and eggs. Perhaps we could give our godchildren a fresh farm egg and some slices of bacon for breakfast on that day, to be cooked by themselves if they are old enough. This gift should include an explanation of the origin of this tradition.

Pancake Day is still celebrated in many parts of the country and children can have great fun making and tossing their own. There is a story that goes back to Saxon times of a village in Yorkshire that was overrun by Danes. The men fled into the forest leaving the women to cope with the invaders! However the women decided to overthrow their masters and formed a plan to kill them. For total success each woman had to agree to the plan, so a signal was arranged. Everyone was to cook pancakes for the meal the day before Ash Wednesday. There was a wonderful smell of pancakes cooking from every kitchen fireplace and the hungry Danes suspecting nothing, sat down to a meal of pancakes sweetened with honey and flavoured with the juice of berries. In the early hours of Ash Wednesday they were killed by the women using sharp kitchen knives. The news spread to their husbands in the forest, and when they came out of hiding their wives cooked them pancakes too. Eating pancakes became a yearly way to celebrate their freedom. Perhaps on Pancake Day we could encourage our godchildren and their families to pray for people who are not free, especially those in prison for their faith.

Lent

Lent has traditionally been a time of abstinence and many children used to 'give up' something for Lent, usually sweets. Sadly this idea is not popular these days but godparents are in a position to help with some positive thinking in this area. My initial experience of being filled with the Holy Spirit came after 'fasting' from my viewing of television during Lent one year. Denying ourselves something should be undertaken in order to give ourselves something else. Children can be encouraged to do without sweets or comics and the pocket money thus saved could be divided and half put into a special box for hungry children or other needy people, and the rest into another box for spending at Easter. Godparents and parents should set the children a good example in this area of self-denial. If the whole family enters into the spirit of Lent then it is much easier for each member to keep to their commitment—six weeks is a long time to 'go it alone'!

Many adults use Lenten Courses and special books: I found *A Feast For Lent* by Delia Smith[1] very helpful. Something for older children and their parents is to arrange a viewing of the video Jesus of Nazareth. This could be organised on a number of evenings over Lent culminating in the events of Easter shown on Easter afternoon if the weather is not suitable for outdoor activities. Most video shops rent the three video's that make up the film, or you may know someone who has bought these and would lend them to you.

Fasting from food has been a tradition in the church for many generations and with the number of people who are overweight in the West today many Christians could use Lent to discipline themselves to eat less. This time could be used for a family to sit down and discuss its eating habits and see if there are things which need to be altered so that we honour our bodies as temples of God's Holy Spirit. Paul, writing to the Church in Corinth asks 'Do you not know that your body is a temple of the Holy Spirit within you, which you have from God?' He goes on to remind them 'You are not your own; you were bought with a price. So glorify God in your body' (1 Cor 6:19–20). Godparents who are trained in nutrition would have valuable things to contribute here.

Doing without a meal releases time to spend in prayer and sharpens our antennae in the things of the Spirit and sometimes the call of God in our lives. Godparents in Lent could covenant with God to do without a certain meal regularly and use the time to pray for their god-children. It is often in these times that the Holy Spirit can give insights and directions for praying which have very beneficial effects on the children.

Mothering Sunday

The fourth Sunday in Lent is known as Mothering Sunday. The name probably derives from the tradition of people coming together from their own churches to worship at the 'Mother' church—usually a cathedral or large parish church. The whole family attended the service and then went home to enjoy a dinner of roast lamb or veal followed by rice pudding, fig pie or plum pudding. It was washed down with mulled ale. The children drank frumenty which was made of wheat grains boiled in milk with sugar and spices added.

Out of this came the idea of honouring the mother of the family. Young people who worked away from home were given the day off to visit their mothers. They usually took a gift of wild flowers picked on the way and a cake they had baked, called simnel. Gifts of flowers are given by children to their mothers during Mothering Sunday services all over the country. Sometimes cards with suitable verses are substituted if flowers are scarce in gardens and hedgerows or too expensive to buy. Parents can encourage their children to give flowers or a card to their godmothers on this day too.

This could be a time for godparents to be available to those, perhaps older children, whose relationship with their mothers is strained. Lending a listening ear and offering ministry can help to heal the wounds in families. If you are a godparent to a child without a father then taking that child to the shops to buy something for their mother would be greatly appreciated.

Palm Sunday

Holy Week starts with Palm Sunday when the church remembers the triumphal entry of Jesus into Jerusalem on a donkey. In Roman times commanders of triumphant armies rode in their victory procession on a donkey. Many congregations decorate their churches with palm branches or 'pussy' willows, and crosses made

out of palm fronds are given out. In our church we used
to reserve this custom for the Good Friday Family Service, it seemed a more appropriate symbol for that day
and was also an added incentive to get children and their
parents to come to the service! The crosses were also
given out in the afternoon when we have three half-hour
(in some churches it is three hours) meditations on the
cross.

There is a lovely modern hymn that captures the spirit
of celebration of Palm Sunday which many of my godchildren enjoy as it has actions to accompany it. The title
is 'Hosanna, Lord' and it is published on cassette, record
and sheet music by Celebration Services and available
from Christian bookshops. A member of our congregation wrote another song that older children might enjoy
called 'Lift up your heads'. This was recorded on the
record 'With Thanksgiving' and is also in the song book
of the same title[2].

Maundy Thursday

On Maundy Thursday the church commemorates the
loving act of Jesus when he washed the feet of his disciples at the last supper. The word is derived from the
Latin *mandatum* meaning 'a commandment'. The opening words of the service begin with the words of Jesus 'A
new commandment I give unto you that you love one
another.' These words have been set to music in a modern composition and are used in many churches.

A tradition developed in England whereby the Mon-
arch would publicly wash the feet of a number of poor
men and give them a gift. When Edward III was fifty
years old he gave slippers to fifty poor men. This was the
origin of the sovereign giving the equivalent number of
gifts for his/her age. The washing of feet was discon-

tinued in 1730 although the Lord High Almoner and his assistants still wear linen towels as a reminder.

There are quite a number of postcards of the Queen distributing Maundy money available that can be sent to godchildren, and perhaps they could be encouraged to give one penny for every year of their age to a child not so well off as themselves. This could be distributed through Save The Children Fund, the Church of England Children's Society or Dr Barnardo's for example. If you have a video you could record the Maundy Service for your godchildren and invite them round to watch it together.

The significance of the foot washing ceremony is lost in modern times when we have pavements to walk on and only wear sandals in the summer. In order to help a group of children at our church to understand something of this without using basins of water that could be knocked over with the ensuing flood, I asked the girls to bring their hairbrushes to the next meeting. After getting them into pairs I told them to brush each others hair and to do so lovingly and carefully. The boys were instructed to take off and put on each others shoes. It was a very significant time for me and for one small boy; for weeks I had had a great deal of difficulty with him and I often went home and wept with frustration. I asked the Lord repeatedly for help to find a solution. The evening we were celebrating the 'foot washing' by using hair brushes and shoes, he came to me in tears. He was totally frustrated by his partner who refused to co-operate in having his shoes put on. I was then able to share with him that he made me just as frustrated when he did not co-operate with me and I often went home in tears. He looked at me with astonishment as understanding dawned and things rapidly improved after that!

Some churches recall the last meal Jesus shared with his disciples by holding a Communion Service on the evening of Maundy Thursday and this is something that older godchildren and their parents should be encouraged to go to.

Many of the great painters and wood carvers of old depicted the Last Supper and godchildren with an interest in art would probably enjoy a library book with some of these works of art to look at. If you are travelling abroad and visit churches and art galleries it is often possible to buy postcards with these masterpieces on them. A child living in Brazil sent me a lovely wall hanging of the Last Supper in batik.

Good Friday

In our church we hold a Family Service on Good Friday morning and everyone is given a palm cross. The meaning of the death of Jesus can be explained simply to children and their parents through the use of this visual aid.

Most churches also have services of meditation when the time Jesus spent on the cross is remembered, and these services are suitable for godchildren who are older and have been confirmed.

On Good Friday it is traditional to eat hot cross buns. This is one of those traditions taken from pagans and used by Christians to affirm their new faith. In pre-Christian times pagans offered their god Zeus a cake baked in the form of a bull with a cross on it to represent its horns. The Romans in Britain made spiced buns marked with a cross. On Good Friday, 1361, a monk made some small spiced cakes to be distributed to the poor at St Albans. It was a popular act and a new tradition was established. Godparents could establish a 'tradition' by inviting godchildren to tea on Good Friday to eat hot cross buns. This would make a good opportunity to talk through all that had been learned in the church services about the death of Jesus—or spend some time looking at the Bible account of this part of the Easter story.

Easter Day

Easter Day is a time for great celebration—God raised Jesus to life. He had accepted the death of his son as payment for the debt of our sins. The first disciples found it very difficult to believe and they took a little persuading that Jesus was not a ghost! Easter hymns are full of praise, and we always make a special set of banners and hang them on the pillars in church. We have choreographed many dances to the songs we sing in our services as well as using dances from Israel, and the children and adults dance outside before the service. Visitors to York are intrigued by what they see and often join us for the service!

One Easter morning we released lots of balloons with labels bearing the Easter message. They soared up past the towers of the Minster and it was a wonderful symbol of the resurrection. This event helped many of the children to realise how special Easter Day is. This Easter there was a new banner showing balloons rising through clouds with the words 'Christ Has Set Us Free'. Every child brought a balloon to their children's meeting and they were tied in large clusters to the six pillars in the church. The banner and the balloons spoke clearly of a celebration and many people were helped to enter into the joy of Easter.

An Easter garden is a marvellous teaching aid for children. A small model of the garden where the body of

Jesus was buried is made on a plate or in a shallow bowl. Moss makes it a lush green place, with twigs and flowers to make it into a garden. A 'tomb' is made with stones, and one large one is 'rolled away' to show that Jesus is no longer dead but alive! Godparents can show their god-children how to make one of these 'gardens' and help them search for beautiful mosses and other suitable greenery.

The giving of Easter Eggs has been a traditional way to celebrate the end of the long Lenten fast. This custom can be traced back long before the birth of Christ! In ancient China, 900 BC, eggs were decorated and used in festivals celebrating the return of spring and the conti-nuance of life from an object that appeared to be 'dead'. Early man believed the egg represented life and those who possessed them would enjoy health and fortune and they gave them as gifts each Spring. Christians adopted the symbolism to denote the rising of Christ from the dead bringing the gift of eternal life to all those who accepted him as Lord and Saviour.

Before the advent of chocolate in solid form, about 150 years ago, people usually hard-boiled their eggs in water to which plants had been added which would dye them. Many children today have great fun boiling and dyeing eggs and decorating them. There are now kits on the market to help, but in libraries books can be found with helpful instructions on the use of plants for colour-ing eggs. It is great fun to gather plants and use them for dyes. When I was a child I remember going with a lot of my school friends to a hill above the town and rolling our eggs down the hill to see which covered the most ground and remained intact. Then everyone would sit down and eat their eggs. Sometimes there was little left that was edible! This tradition is thought to commemorate the rolling of the stone away from the tomb on Easter morning. It is something in which the whole family, including godparents and friends, can participate.

Chocolate eggs come in all sort of imaginative wrappings today and I enjoy choosing them for my godchildren. Alternatively you can buy egg moulds and make your own creations. Sometimes for a change I give my godchildren a few small chocolate eggs and a book or cassette which relates to the events of Easter. If your godchildren tend to receive lots of chocolate eggs there are lovely decorated cardboard eggs on the market which can be filled with a present of your choice. Some children I know have an arrangement with their godparent to return the empty cardboard egg for it to be refilled each year!

Whitsunday

Whitsunday is celebrated on the seventh Sunday after Easter Day. The festival commemorates the coming of the Holy Spirit to the disciples together with several women, including the mother of Jesus and other relatives.

The account of this is found in the New Testament in the second chapter of the Acts of the Apostles. Before Jesus ascended into heaven he left instructions with his disciples to wait in Jerusalem because they were to receive power when the Holy Spirit came upon them. This power was needed to enable them to carry on the work that Jesus had begun during his time on earth, when he set about establishing the kingdom of God.

The disciples and others had gathered in an upper room on the Day of Pentecost. This was a feast on which the Jews celebrated the giving of the Ten Commandments on Mount Sinai.

> ...when suddenly they heard what sounded like a powerful wind from heaven, the noise of which filled the entire house in which they were sitting; and something appeared to them that seemed like tongues of fire; these separated and came to rest on the head of each of them. They were all filled with the Holy Spirit and began to speak in foreign languages as the Spirit gave them the gift of speech (Acts 2:1–4).

This caused quite a commotion and the many different nationalities living in Jerusalem who had rushed to see what was happening concluded that they must be drunk, even though it was only nine o'clock in the morning! They were astonished to hear Galileans speaking in the known languages of the day and all talking about the marvels of God.

Peter took advantage of the situation. He unfolded all the teaching in the Old Testament about which they were familiar, but put them into the context of the life and ministry of Jesus. About three thousand people came to believe that Jesus was indeed the Messiah they had been promised. It was a day of great excitement in Jerusalem. The church was born.

The origin of the word *Whit* may mean White Sunday. Traditional white robes were worn by adults being baptised and confirmed at Easter and Whitsun in earlier centuries. Iceland and Norway were countries to which Britain sent missionaries and the literal translation of Whitsun in both languages is 'white'. White may also refer to the tradition of the rich giving all their milk to the poor on Whitsunday.

Another explanation is that it may have come from the Anglo-Saxon word *Hwit* or *Wit*; the giving of 'wit' to the disciples when they were empowered to speak in languages they had never learnt on the Day of Pentecost.

In recent years, with what has come to be called the 'Charismatic Renewal', there has been a resurgence of the gifts of the Spirit. As godparents it is important that we have some understanding of the work of the Holy Spirit so that we can instruct our godchildren.

The best and most effective way to instruct is from first hand experience. In the Bible Paul gives details of the gifts of the Spirit in his first letter to the church in Corinth (1 Cor 12 and 14). It is also good to read how the first disciples used these gifts and saw them given to others; accounts of these events can be found in the Acts of the Apostles. (Some people feel a more appropriate title for this part of the Bible would be 'The Acts of the Holy Spirit'.)

Bishops in the Church of England lay their hands on Confirmation candidates so that they may be filled with the Holy Spirit; sometimes God works quite directly without the help of other Christians. I was asking God one day to give me a gift of faith so that I could please him when something very dramatic happened—I was filled with the Spirit and spoke in tongues. I had no idea what had happened and did not have any words to explain it until my husband-to-be lent me a booklet to read as part of my Confirmation preparation classes.

If we ourselves have not yet experienced the super-natural working of the Holy Spirit in our lives we should ask a friend or minister to pray and lay hands on us so that we might be empowered to receive the gifts of the Spirit. Sometimes people are too embarrassed or shy to ask for others to pray for them and rely on God to fill or baptise them with the Spirit secretly. This rarely happens, the very fact of acknowledging our need and plucking up courage to ask for prayer prepares us to receive the Holy Spirit in this special way.

Children can acknowledge the presence of Jesus at a very early age through the work of the Holy Spirit; even before they are born, and as parents and godparents we should remember this. John the Baptist leapt in his mother's womb when his aunt, the Virgin Mary, visited their house when she too was pregnant with her son, Jesus. The effect on Elizabeth was that she was filled with the Holy Spirit and began to prophesy. What a meeting! Pregnancy can be a time to experience the presence of the Holy Spirit in a new way.

When the angel Gabriel told the Virgin Mary 'The Lord is with you' she was frightened. The angel had to tell her not to be afraid. We can be just as anxious and questioning when faced with the supernatural works of God. However, Mary was able to respond humbly and say 'I am the handmaid of the Lord...let what you have said be done to me' (Lk 1:38). As godparents we need to have the same attitude—being available to God so that the Holy Spirit can come upon us and equip us to serve our godchildren and their parents with all the gifts of the Spirit.

If I am godparent to one child in a family and know them well, I pray and minister to all subsequent children before they are born. The parents of your godchildren, too, should not be forgotten. Simeon, who lived in Jerusalem in the time of Jesus, was a devout man and the Holy Spirit rested upon him (Lk 2:25). He knew through a revelation of the Holy Spirit that he would see the Messiah before he died. He was prompted by the Spirit to go to the Temple on the very day that Mary and

Joseph brought Jesus to be circumcised. Taking Jesus in his arms he gave thanks to God (the words he used are now incorporated into the Evening Prayer service and known as the *Nunc Dimittis*). Mary and Joseph were wondering what was happening so he turned to them and blessed them and gave Mary a prophecy:

> You see this child: he is destined for the fall and for the rising of many in Israel, destined to be a sign that is rejected—and a sword will pierce your own soul too—so that the secret thoughts of many may be laid bare (Lk 2:34–35).

What a help that must have been to Mary in the years that lay ahead when people began to reject her son and finally arranged for him to be crucified by the Romans.

One of the gifts of the Spirit is the ability to prophesy. To tell people what God wants them to know. I asked God for this gift not long after coming to York. Paul urges Christians to desire the gifts of the Spirit, especially that of prophecy. He said in 1 Cor 14:3 that the person who prophesies 'talk(s) to other people, to their improvement, their encouragement and their consolation'. Another translation adds that prophecy edifies the church.

I constantly ask God for words of encouragement, consolation and improvement for the parents of my godchildren in the form of prophecy. These are usually given to me when I am laying hands on them, either at the Communion rail, in house meetings or when praying privately with them. I have noticed that quite a few times the prophecies include references to their children.

At times I will be asked to pray for my godchildren if they are sick or experiencing some difficulty at home or at school. It is much easier to pray for small children when they are asleep—they are rarely quiet or still when awake! If there is any difficulty getting a child to co-operate, whatever the age, then wait until they are asleep. I stand or sit beside their bed and hold my hand out over their heads asking the Holy Spirit to come upon them. I then wait to see what he will do. I ask the Lord to give me any words of knowledge or wisdom that I need in order to pray for healing effectively. A word of knowledge will pinpoint the cause of the trouble. A word of wisdom will give direction when you don't know how to proceed. Both these are gifts of the Holy Spirit.

The gifts of the Spirit are given to us so that we can bring God's blessings to others. However, God is not unmindful of the needs of those who minister for their own refreshment. One of the gifts of the Spirit is given for precisely this reason, the gift of tongues. The tongue may be a known language in the world or one known by the angels. Without an interpretation the person speaking will not understand what they are saying. Only God will. The effect of using this given language is to edify the person who is speaking and should be used in private or while ministering to a person (usually not out loud). Paul explains this in 1 Cor 14:4. Paul himself spoke in tongues a great deal—more than those to whom he was writing in Corinth.

I use the gift constantly: both privately and in ministry. I find it very refreshing and relaxing. It also seems to help me to hear instructions from God through the Holy Spirit when I have come to an impasse in a time of ministry.

Many children I know have been given this gift by God. I know of one little girl who asked her parents 'Why do I keep saying strange words when I talk to Jesus?' They would find her skipping along the road talking away in tongues quite happily!

If it is a normal part of a family's experience then the gift will probably be used frequently, but in other families these particular gifts may not be part and parcel of their Christian experience. It is always difficult to be disciplined in the use of a gift from God, particularly if there are not others around with the same experience to encourage you.

Most of the children in our church hear the gift of tongues first in the Family Service when we worship God together by singing in tongues. When we do this we have noticed that the children become very quiet and babies can fall asleep. The whole incident will cause questions to be asked by the children. This is the time to tell them about the Holy Spirit and the presents he brings. Parents in our church may well invite godparents to join with them in praying for the children to be filled with the Spirit and be given the gift of tongues.

Some parents, sadly, believe that the giving of a gift of the Spirit to their child has turned the child into someone special, putting them on a pedestal. They can begin to expect far too much from these children. Gifts are not a sign of spiritual maturity, they are given to the youngest of Christians! Gifts are not given to make us special—we *are* special. Our water baptism is a sign of that. We have to learn to grow in the fruit of the Spirit—love, joy, peace, patience, kindness, goodness, trustfulness, gentleness and self-control—to be fully mature in Christ. God loves us and welcomes us into his family. What greater privilege can there be than that?

9

Harvest

The next festival in the church's year is Harvest.
Churches all over the world hold Harvest Festivals and
sing well-loved harvest hymns. Displays of all kinds of
fruit and vegetables and autumn flowers decorate the
church. Since the advent of the combine harvester
sheaves of corn or wheat are no longer seen, but bales of
straw provide areas on which to lay the gifts children are
encouraged to bring. These will be distributed to elderly
people in the parish after the service. Gifts are usually of
fruit, vegetables, tinned food, eggs, home-made jams
and jellies and other harvest produce.

This tradition was only introduced in the middle of the
last century. Farm labourers were paid as much as £5 in
gold sovereigns for their labours at harvest time. These
coins were called 'Hossmen' because they were
imprinted with a picture of St George, riding on a horse,
and the dragon. This money was supposed to last

through the leaner days of winter when there was little paid work. However, much of it was spent in the ale houses and families went hungry.

In an attempt to reverse this trend local clergy began to encourage people to bring a sample of their harvest produce to church for a service of thanksgiving. I am sure many wives and children were glad when this custom became so popular! It has now become part of the Christian calendar.

It is much more rewarding to encourage children to save some of their own pocket money to buy a harvest gift rather than just hand them something from the larder. An outing to pick blackberries for bramble jelly is something for godparents to organise—godfathers with walking sticks would be very useful here as the best berries are always out of reach! Some years there is a glut of apples and these can be turned into jelly too. Elderly people often prefer to eat jelly rather than jam which has pips in it. Many elderly people live on their own, so try and find small jam jars as a large pot can take a long time to get through. Also small jars are much less likely to be dropped when they are taken up to the front on Harvest Sunday!

I found some lovely postcards in the Medici range with drawings of animals collecting brambles. I plan to send these, plus a recipe, to some of my godchildren when the berries are ripe as an encouragement for them to gather enough to make jelly for Harvest gifts. Younger godchildren could be involved by cutting out cloth tops to cover the jars in pretty material.

One family I know keep hens and the children bring fresh eggs to church as their gift. If small children want to bring eggs it is much better to put them in a basket with plenty of padding, rather than in the usual egg carton. The type of basket supplied when you pick your own fruit at berry farms, or those that have held mush-rooms, have handles to hold and so are less likely to be dropped!

If a posy of flowers is added for decoration, then wrap the stalks in wet cotton wool covered with a polythene bag. This can then be disguised with silver paper or material. This will prevent them from dying before they can be distributed the next day.

Children love planting seeds and a packet of seeds given in April with the idea of growing the contents for Harvest would be an idea. Edibles are not always so easy to grow but radishes have a good record, and tomatoes are a very acceptable gift for Harvest.

Many men who are not interested in a garden are very happy in their greenhouses. Perhaps a child could be given a greenhouse plant to look after. A godfather's skills could be shared with his godchild and a sample of their combined labours brought in thanksgiving to God on Harvest Sunday.

In pagan Britain people believed that the corn spirit lived in the last sheaf of corn. In order to preserve it and allow it to be reborn the next Spring they made idols using the corn stalks. These were then hung in their houses for protection from evil spirits and diseases through the winter. This superstition is not now con-nected with the making of 'corn dollies' as they are called. There is no inherent evil in the corn stalks or the patterns that can be made with them and many people make these 'dollies' as a traditional craft. It is a skill that children can learn too and my own children had great enjoyment creating different patterns from corn stalks and giving them as presents to grandparents at Harvest time.

There is also the harvest of the sea. Children living near the coast could make and paint fishes. These could then be attached to a dark blue background. If the material used has an open weave then when it is hung up with the fish on it an impression is created of the fish swimming in the water.

If godparents are able to spend time helping their godchildren appreciate God's wonderful provision for us, then the Harvest Festival will be an occasion for real thanksgiving for these children.

10

Saints' Days

Saints' Days are not celebrated in the Protestant church as they are in the Roman Catholic church, but countries have adopted certain Christians as Patron Saints. England commemorates St George on 23rd April; Scotland commemorates St Andrew on 30th November; Wales commemorates St David's Day on 1st March and Ireland has St Patrick's Day on 17th March.

Finding out the history of these people is a fascinating exercise, and composing it into something understandable for your godchildren's interest is a worthwhile task. Postcards about the saint together with a short history could be sent to a godchild on that special day. The child could be encouraged to keep a scrap book of them, adding anything they have found to it as well.

Churches are often named after Christians who have made a special contribution to the spreading of Christianity and they are often remembered in Patronal Festivals. The church my husband and I came to serve in York is called St Cuthbert. He is remembered on 20th March. Now that two of my York godchildren are older I plan to tell them the story of St Cuthbert on this particular day, and also some of the things I remember of our early days in St Cuthbert's Church. Composing a questionnaire for godchildren to fill in would gain their interest, or if they were older they could do their own 'research' and be suitably rewarded for their efforts. Knowing the history of their own church helps children to take a keener interest in coming to the services.

There is one saint's day that is celebrated by many people—St Valentine's Day! This festival started with a Christian foundation but has now become secularised and commercialised, and on 14th February each year people send cards and gifts to those they love, usually anonymously.

Valentine lived during the reign of Claudius II. He was well known as a preacher and was arrested and imprisoned because of his loyalty to Jesus Christ. Flogging and stoning could not induce him to renounce his faith. His jailor was so impressed by his commitment that he brought his blind daughter to the prison so that Valentine could pray for her. She received her sight and became a follower of Christ.

Claudius condemned Valentine to death as he could see that nothing would destroy his faith and on the night before he was to be beheaded Valentine wrote a letter to the jailer's daughter. In it he encouraged her to pray, witness and be faithful to the Lord. It concluded with three words, 'From your Valentine'. The date was 14th February, AD 270.

St Valentine's Day is a reminder of the unswerving love that a disciple of Jesus had for his Master—for 'love is strong as death' (Song 8:6).

We hear nothing more of the jailor's daughter and the struggles she may have had to follow Christ in a hostile environment. But there is a story of another little girl which I have sent to some of my godchildren on Valentine's Day. She came from Wales and her name was Mary Jones. Mary wanted to have a Bible of her own and the story recounts the struggles she had to save enough money and then her walk for miles and miles to buy one.

St Francis of Assisi is another well-known saint. He came from a wealthy Italian family, but during the war between Assisi and the neighbouring town of Perugia he was captured and held prisoner for a year. He longed to return to the life of pleasure to which he was accustomed. However, when he was released he found he was discontented. He decided to go to war again and fight the Germans who were invading Italy, but the night before he left God spoke to him in a dream and he abandoned his plans.

He found he was seeing people with new eyes. Not those who had been his friends—the noble and wealthy—but those who were poor. He gave away all his money and possessions and served the sick and the poor. He gathered others to help him and founded the Franciscan religious order in Assisi in 1208.

Francis taught that Christians should show that they were followers of Jesus Christ by loving one another—just as Jesus had commanded:

> I give you a new commandment:
> love one another;
> just as I have loved you,
> you must love one another.
> By this love you have for one another,
> everyone will know that you are my disciples (Jn 13:34–35).

Many churches today sing a lovely new hymn called 'The

Prayer of Saint Francis'—the first line is 'Make me a channel of your peace'. It would be a good song to introduce to a godchild when he or she is working on a topic at school on 'Peace' or the 'Nuclear Issue'.

Francis' favourite festival was Christmas. He was the first to have a crib in church to help people understand the great truth that 'Love came down at Christmas'. As St Francis' Day is on 4th October it is not too early to give a godchild one of the lovely Nativity sets made of card that need to be coloured in and cut out. It would give the child plenty of time before the Christmas rush starts—though they have probably already begun preparations if they are at school!

However, Francis is mostly remembered for his great love of creation—especially birds and animals. One way to commemorate this would be to give one's godchild information about societies that encourage care for birds and animals. The Royal Society for the Protection of Birds is well-known, as is the World Wildlife Fund. These societies often send out catalogues in the months before Christmas and all gifts bought through them go towards the society's funds. Giving a catalogue on 4th October might encourage a child to support the society himself.

Starting a project to build a bird table is another practical idea to begin in October. Hopefully it would be ready to provide food for hungry birds in winter and give the child an opportunity to observe them.

Perhaps on the nearest Saturday to St Francis' Day for those children who are at school, an outing to a zoo would be appropriate. There is a wonderful Museum of Farming near York where farm animals can be seen at close quarters which is an ideal place to visit to celebrate St Francis' Day. I know quite a few godmothers in our congregation who have spent lovely days there with their godchildren. In a number of large cities there are small-holdings where children can observe and help to feed farm animals.

Animals have a high profile in the Bible story of Noah and the ark (Gen 6–8). If all the information about St Francis himself has been exhausted then this is something that can provide ideas for things to do in October.

We need to remember, of course, that all Christians are saints. Paul and Timothy open their letter to the church in Philippi with these words:

> From Paul and Timothy, servants of Christ Jesus, to all the saints in Christ Jesus, together with their presiding elders and deacons. We wish you the grace and peace of God our Father and of the Lord Jesus Christ (Phil 1:1–2).

Paul says the same in his other letters.

In every age there have been men and women who have loved Christ and endeavoured to follow him. Some are well-remembered and others not known. One of our tasks as parents and godparents is by encouragement and example to show our children how to do the same.

In Conclusion

My hope is, that in sharing what I am learning, I will have encouraged parents and godparents alike. It is the children who will carry forward the faith of Christ to the generations to come. How important it is for us to pass on that faith to them in meaningful ways. To make ways for them to serve the church from their childhood. Children are excluded from so much in the church and we as parents and godparents need to be open to the Holy Spirit so that we can discover how to open doors wide and let them in.

Jesus said:

"Let the little children come to me; do not stop them; for it is to such as these that the kingdom of God belongs. I tell you solemnly, anyone who does not welcome the kingdom of God like a little child will never enter it." Then he put his arms round them, laid his hands on them and gave them his blessing (Mk 10:14–16).

Notes

Chapter 2

1 Mary E. Cullen (editor), *My Faith* (Marshall Pickering: Basingstoke 1986).
2 *Jesus Then And Now*, Video by David Watson, book by David Watson and Simon Jenkins (Lion: Tring 1983).
3 Christian Video Guide obtainable from Elm House Christian Communications Ltd, 37 Elm Road, New Malden, Surrey KT3 3HB.
4 James Dobson, *Dare to Discipline* (Kingsway: Eastbourne, 1986) and *Discipline While You Can* (Kingsway: Eastbourne, 1978).
5 Maggie Durran, *Hello, I'm a Person Too* (Kingsway: Eastbourne, 1984).
6 Francis MacNutt, *The Prayer That Heals* (Hodder & Stoughton: London, 1966).
7 Joyce Huggett, *Marriage On The Mend* (Kingsway: Eastbourne, 1987) and *Conflict: Friend or Foe* (Kingsway: Eastbourne, 1984).
8 Floyd McClung, *The Father Heart of God* (Kingsway: Eastbourne, 1985).

9 Audiotapes by the author available from the St
   Cuthbert's Tape Library, Peaseholme Green,
   York.

Chapter 3

1 *The Lord is Here* (Collins: Glasgow, 1981).

Chapter 5

1 'I Spy' books published by 'I Spy Books', Partridge
   Green, Horsham.

Chapter 6

1 My Faith, *op cit.*

2 David Watson, *One In The Spirit* (Hodder &
   Stoughton: London, 1973).

3 David Watson, *Be Filled With The Spirit* (Kingsway, Falcon: Eastbourne 1982).

4 Greenbelt Festivals, 11 Uxbridge St., London W8
   7TA.

5 Horizons Mission Without Bounds, 2a Glanmor
   Rd, Llanelli, Dyfed SA15 1DB.

6 CYFA–Pathfinder Ventures Ltd, Falcon Court, 32
   Fleet St., London EC4Y 1DB.

7 Crusaders, Crusade House, 2 Romelands Hill, St
   Albans, Herts AL3 3ET.

Chapter 7

1 Bible Lands Society, PO Box 50, High Wycombe,
   Bucks HP15 7QU.

Chapter 8

1 Delia Smith, *A Feast For Lent* (The Bible Reading
   Fellowship: London, 1983).

2 'With Thanksgiving' record and songbook obtainable from St Cuthbert's Centre, Peaseholm Green,
   York.